# Audit Report

Report Number: OIG-SBLF-13-001

STATE SMALL BUSINESS CREDIT INITIATIVE: Vermont's Use of Federal Funds for Capital Access and Credit Support Programs

November 30, 2012

# Office of Inspector General

Department of the Treasury

# Contents

Results In Brief .................................................................................................................... 2
Background ........................................................................................................................ 4
   State of Vermont's Participation in the SSBCI ............................................................. 5
      Vermont Capital Access Program .............................................................................. 5
      Commercial Loan Participation Program .................................................................. 6
      Technology Loan Participation Program .................................................................. 6
      Small Business Participation Program ...................................................................... 7
Accounting Practices for Vermont's Interest Rate Subsidy Program Were Non-Compliant ............... 7
Administrative Costs Charged to SSBCI Were Not Allowable or Allocable ........................... 10
Vermont Did Not Obtain Borrower and Lender Assurances at Loan Closing ......................... 11
Recommendations ........................................................................................................... 14
Appendix 1: Objective, Scope, and Methodology ........................................................... 17
Appendix 2: Management Response ............................................................................... 19
Appendix 3: Major Contributors ...................................................................................... 25
Appendix 4: Distribution List ........................................................................................... 26

# Abbreviations

   OIG          Office of Inspector General
   OMB         Office of Management and Budget
   SSBCI       State Small Business Credit Initiative
   The Act     Small Business Jobs Act of 2010
   VCAP       Vermont Capital Access Program
   VEDA       Vermont Economic Development Authority

# OIG

*The Department of the Treasury*
*Office of Inspector General*

# Audit Report

November 30, 2012

Don Graves, Jr.
Deputy Assistant Secretary for Small Business, Housing, and Community Development

This report presents the results of our audit of the State of Vermont's use of funds awarded under the State Small Business Credit Initiative (SSBCI), which was established by the Small Business Jobs Act of 2010 (the Act). Vermont was awarded $13,168,350 in March 2011, which was allocated to four small business programs: the Financial Access Program ($1,037,700), the Commercial Participation Program, ($5,883,730), the Technology Participation Program ($2,957,430), and the Small Business Participation Program ($3,289,490). On May 26, 2011, the State received $4,345,556, the first distribution of the awarded funds and as of March 31, 2012, had obligated or spent $2,582,172.

The Act requires the Treasury Office of Inspector General (OIG) to conduct audits of the use of funds made available under SSBCI and to identify any instances of reckless or intentional misuse. Treasury has defined reckless misuse as a use of funds that the participating state or administering entity should have known was unauthorized or prohibited, and which is a highly unreasonable departure or willful disregard from the standards of ordinary care. Intentional misuse is any unauthorized or prohibited use of funds that the participating state or its administering entity knew was unauthorized or prohibited.

Our audit objective was to test participant compliance with program requirements and prohibitions to identify any reckless or intentional misuse of funds.

To test participant compliance, we reviewed a statistical sample of 26 loans enrolled in Vermont's SSBCI programs as of December 31, 2011. We reviewed the loans to determine whether they complied with program requirements for loan use, capital at risk, and other restrictions. We also reviewed the administrative costs charged against SSBCI funds related to these programs to ensure those administrative costs were accurate and supported in accordance with Treasury Guidelines and Office of Management and Budget (OMB) Circular A-87, *Cost Principles for State, Local, and Indian Tribal Government*.[1] We visited the offices of the Vermont Economic Development Authority (VEDA), the administrative entity with responsibility for the use of SSBCI funds in Vermont. All loan files sampled from the applicable lending institutions were directly forwarded to us electronically or provided to us on site at VEDA. Appendix 1 contains a more detailed description of our audit objectives, scope, and methodology.

We conducted our audit from June to October 2012 in accordance with Government Auditing Standards. Those standards require that we plan and perform the audit to obtain sufficient, appropriate evidence to provide a reasonable basis for our findings and conclusions based on our audit objectives. We believe that the evidence obtained to address our audit objectives provides a reasonable basis for our findings and conclusions.

## Results In Brief

We determined that accounting practices for Vermont's interest rate subsidy program did not comply with the requirements established by its Allocation Agreement. The Agreement requires the State to adequately account for the application of funds for federally sponsored activities. Interest rate subsidies financed with SSBCI funds are estimated, and therefore VEDA's quarterly reports to Treasury do not reflect the State's actual use of funds for the program. Without reporting the actual use of funds, the State cannot provide Treasury with accurate information for measuring the leverage achieved with

---

[1] Office of Management and Budget Circular Number A-87, revised May 10, 2004.

SSBCI funds. In addition, revenue generated by SSBCI funds is returned to VEDA's operating account, and not recorded in VEDA's SSBCI sub-account, as required by SSBCI Policy Guidelines. Vermont's SSBCI application described the interest rate subsidy in detail such that Treasury officials should have been aware of the potential accounting complexities. However, Treasury did not evaluate the adequacy of states' accounting practices when approving state programs for SSBCI funding. Once the interest rate subsidy program was approved, Vermont was responsible for adequately accounting for the application of SSBCI funds. Because the State did not do this, it may have breached its Allocation Agreement.

Further, we found that $216,820 in administrative costs charged to the SSBCI program as of March 31, 2012, did not comply with program guidance. Additionally, although borrower and/or lender assurances, which are key requirements of the program, were compliant with SSBCI Policy Guidelines by the conclusion of our audit fieldwork, they were incomplete at the time of loan closing for 20, or 77 percent, of the 26 loans sampled. Despite the incomplete assurances, the State inaccurately certified in September 2011 and December 2011 that it was in compliance with program requirements. Because the State failed to comply with Section 4.1 of its Allocation Agreement with Treasury and made compliance certifications that were materially inaccurate, Treasury may consider such findings to constitute a general event of default of Vermont's Allocation Agreement.

We recommended that Treasury disallow $216,820 of administrative expenses claimed by Vermont unless the State can submit documentation in accordance with OMB Circular A-87 supporting those expenses and disallow future administrative expenses until the State demonstrates it is tracking direct costs and has a cost allocation plan. Further, we recommended that Treasury require the State to provide a sub-accounting of all the funds transferred in connection with the interest rate subsidy program as well as program income generated from the use of such funds. Finally, Treasury should determine whether Vermont is in general default of its Allocation Agreement due to its non-compliance with accounting and lender/borrower assurance requirements, and whether future funding to the State should be reduced, suspended, or terminated.

Treasury agreed with all of our recommendations and said it would disallow the administrative expenses; require the State to provide a sub-accounting of all expended funds and program income for the interest rate subsidy program; and require the State to provide the necessary documentation before approving additional claims for administrative expenses. Treasury also agreed to determine whether there has been a general event of default under Vermont's Allocation Agreement, and to determine whether reduction, suspension, or termination of funding is warranted.

## Background

SSBCI is a $1.5 billion Treasury program that provides participating states, territories and eligible municipalities with funding to strengthen Capital Access Programs and other credit support programs that provide financial assistance to small businesses and manufacturers. Capital Access Programs provide portfolio insurance for business loans, with a separate loan loss reserve fund for each participating financial institution. Other credit support programs include collateral support, loan participation, loan guarantee, and venture capital programs. Each participating state is required to designate specific departments, agencies, or political subdivisions to implement the programs. Designated state entities may engage in contractual arrangements for the implementation and administration of its state program with an approved program of another state or with a for-profit or not-for-profit entity supervised by the state. These entities use funds to make loans or provide credit access to small businesses.

Primary oversight of the use of SSBCI funds is the responsibility of each participating state. To ensure that funds are properly controlled and expended, the Act requires that Treasury execute an Allocation Agreement with participants setting forth internal controls and compliance and reporting requirements before allocating SSBCI funds. Treasury disburses SSBCI funds to participating states in three parts: the first when the Secretary approves the state for participation, and the second and third after the participating state certifies that it has obligated, transferred, or expended at least 80 percent of the previous disbursement. In addition, the participating state is required to certify that it has complied with all program requirements.

## State of Vermont's Participation in the SSBCI

On March 22, 2011, Treasury approved Vermont's application for participation in SSBCI, and awarded the State a total of $13,168,350. On May 26, 2011, Treasury disbursed the first part of the State's allocation, $4,345,556, and as of the date of this report, had not yet disbursed the second. As of March 31, 2012, Vermont reported that it had obligated or expended a total of $2,582,172, approximately 59 percent of its first disbursement of SSBCI funding. Of this amount, $216,820 had been used to pay administrative costs associated with implementing the enrolled programs.

The Secretary of the Agency of Commerce and Community Development for the State of Vermont designated VEDA as the entity to receive SSBCI funds and administer the program under the Allocation Agreement with Treasury. VEDA operates as an autonomous entity within the State of Vermont. It is authorized to use allocated funds only for the purposes and activities as specified in the Allocation Agreement, including direct and indirect administrative costs. Loans cannot be used to finance business activities prohibited by Treasury's SSBCI Policy Guidelines. SSBCI encourages programs to use risk-based pricing of loans, credit scoring, financial modeling, risk-based capital adequacy standards, reinsurance or other credit risk transfers, and standardized reporting.

The Allocation Agreement between Vermont and Treasury provided funding for four programs: (1) Financial Access Program; (2) Commercial Participation Program; (3) Technology Loan Participation Program; and (4) Small Business Loan Participation Program. The first is a Capital Access Program and the other three are other credit support programs.

### *Vermont Capital Access Program*

In 2011, VEDA launched the Vermont Capital Access Program (VCAP) with SSBCI funds to expand credit to small businesses and promote lending in the State. VCAP is a pooled reserve in which each loan enrolled by a participating financial institution is protected by a reserve account maintained by that institution. The reserve is funded through one-time premiums paid into the reserve in equal parts by the borrower and the lender. VEDA then matches the combined one-time premium with a contribution using SSBCI funds. Each of the financial institutions and borrowers pays a premium of 3 percent of the loan balance, which is matched with a 6 percent premium paid by VCAP.

Vermont's Allocation Agreement provided up to $1,037,700 in SSBCI funds to support VCAP. Of this amount, $14,538 had been expended as of March 31, 2012.

*Commercial Loan Participation Program*

The Commercial Loan Participation Program is an expansion of an interest rate subsidy program that VEDA has operated since fiscal year 2000. The program provides financing for the purchase of land, construction or renovation of facilities, and the purchase and installation of equipment for eligible projects. Using SSBCI funds, the Commercial Loan Participation Program makes direct loans to qualifying commercial enterprises at below-market interest rates. VEDA subsidizes the lower interest rates with SSBCI funds. Vermont's Allocation Agreement provided up to $5,883,730 in SSBCI funds to support this program, of which $1,493,464 had been committed or spent as of March 31, 2012.

*Technology Loan Participation Program*

In 2008, VEDA established a Technology Loan Participation Program through a $500,000 reserve fund supported by the State. The program supports loans to early-stage firms primarily in the information technology and bioscience sectors. The reserve fund covers the additional credit risk inherent in the type of companies targeted, many of which have only intellectual property as loan collateral.

Vermont's Allocation Agreement provides for up to $2,957,430 in SSBCI funds in support of this program. VEDA is using the funds to support interest rate buy-downs or subsidies and to make direct loans to eligible companies. As of March 31, 2012, SSBCI funds totaling

$185,500 had been used or committed to help finance $1,175,000 in loans to three small businesses.

### *Small Business Participation Program*

The Small Business Participation Program makes small business loans of $250,000 or less. The vast majority of program projects involve significant participation from private financial institutions. Vermont's Allocation Agreement provided up to $3,289,490 in SSBCI funds to support this program, of which $671,850 had been used or committed as of March 31, 2012.

## Accounting Practices for Vermont's Interest Rate Subsidy Program Were Non-Compliant

As of March 31, 2012, VEDA reported it had used approximately $931,000 of SSBCI funds to subsidize interest rates on loans awarded under the State's Commercial Loan Participation Program and Small Business Loan Participation Program. The amount of funds reported as used consisted of approximately $71,000 that had been expended for loans enrolled in the program, with the remaining $860,000 committed to service the loan subsidies until maturity.

The portion of the interest rate subsidized with SSBCI funds constitutes the difference between VEDA's target interest rate for each loan, which includes its expected margin, and the actual rate that VEDA expects to charge the borrower, as shown in Table 1 on the following page. The benefit of the program to Vermont's small business borrowers is access to capital at below market interest rates.

**Table 1: Distribution of Interest Rate Subsidy for the Commercial Loan Participation Program and Small Business Loan Program (in Percentages)**

|  | Commercial Participation | Technology Participation | Small Business Participation |
|---|---|---|---|
| VEDA funding cost[a] | 1.50 | 1.50 | 1.50 |
| Normal VEDA margin[b] | 2.75 | 5.25 | 4.00 |
| Borrower rate without SSBCI subsidy | 4.25 | 6.75 | 5.50 |
| Interest rate subsidy financed by SSBCI | -2.25 | 0.00 | -1.50 |
| Rate provided to borrower[c] | 2.00 | 6.75 | 4.00 |

[a] Rate varies each month.
[b] Targeted rate.
[c] May be variable.

Under the Act, to be eligible to use SSBCI funds on other credit support programs, Treasury must consider whether the internal accounting and administrative control systems of that program can adequately safeguard against waste, loss, unauthorized use, and misappropriation. Because Treasury did not evaluate the adequacy of states' accounting practices when approving state programs for SSBCI funding, it accepted the interest subsidy program even though Vermont did not have sufficient accounting practices to meet program requirements.

Two of Vermont's interest rate subsidy program accounting practices were insufficient. First, obligated funds that VEDA reported quarterly to Treasury were based on estimates of what VEDA believed it will expend based on market interest rate projections. VEDA projects the amount of the interest rate subsidy over the life of each loan and shows it as an obligation of SSBCI funds. The amount of the interest rate subsidy and associated use of SSBCI funds on enrolled loans changes each month, depending on VEDA's cost of funds and other factors. As a result, the use of funds reported to Treasury on a quarterly basis was not what was actually used. Without accounting that tracks the actual use of funds for the interest rate subsidy program, the State cannot provide Treasury with accurate information required for measurement of the leverage achieved with SSBCI funds used for interest rate subsidies, as the Act and SSBCI Policy Guidelines require.

Second, VEDA was not posting revenue generated by SSBCI funds to its SSBCI sub-account. Treasury's SSBCI Policy Guidelines require that SSBCI-funded program income, including any returns on capital that is directly generated by SSBCI-supported activity or as a result of the SSBCI funds, must be employed for SSBCI purposes for the 7-year life of the SSBCI program. However, when borrowers make payments on loans with SSBCI-subsidized interest rates, the interest revenue generated is returned to VEDA's operating account and available for other activities managed by VEDA. Treasury's Allocation Agreement allows the comingling of SSBCI funds with other state funds, as long as states maintain a separate sub-account for SSBCI funds. While VEDA maintains such a sub-account; it had not used it to record revenue that was returned. As a result, the State cannot provide Treasury with assurances that SSBCI program income is being properly recycled, as required.

Vermont's SSBCI application described in detail the interest rate subsidy program which, given its complexity, should have raised questions about the adequacy of the State's accounting practices. However, Treasury did not review state accounting practices when approving applicants for the SSBCI program. As a result, Treasury approved the interest subsidy program without knowing whether Vermont's accounting practices were fully compliant with the reporting requirements of the program.

To Treasury's credit, after reviewing Vermont's quarterly reports and a second disbursement request in December 2011, it noted the complexities inherent in VEDA's reporting of the interest rate subsidy. After discussions with Treasury about this issue, Vermont submitted a program modification on May 31, 2012, removing the interest rate subsidy portion of its loan participation programs. While this will prevent funds from being used for interest rate subsidies in the future, Treasury will need to take additional steps to ensure that SSBCI funds already obligated or expended on interest rate subsidies are accurately reported and that any program income from the use of these funds continues to be recycled for SSBCI purposes. Therefore, Treasury will need to notify the State that they must provide a sub-accounting of all the funds transferred in connection with the interest rate subsidy program, as well as program income generated by the use of such funds.

Although Treasury approved the interest rate subsidy program, Vermont was responsible for complying with accounting and administrative oversight requirements once it was approved. Section 4.6(b) of VEDA's Allocation Agreement requires the State to comply with the standards for financial management systems, including internal control requirements specified in the grants management common rule §_.20. These standards require that grant recipients provide "... records that identify adequately the source and application of funds for federally sponsored activities. These records shall contain information pertaining to Federal awards, authorizations, obligations, unobligated balances, assets, outlays, income, and interest." As Vermont's obligation of SSBCI funds for the interest rate subsidy program are estimated, the State is not able to report monthly the actual SSBCI funds employed. Therefore, the State breached the requirements of Section 4.6(b) of its Allocation Agreement, and Treasury should determine whether Vermont is in general default of its agreement. Section 6.1(b) of the Agreement states that general events of default include a material failure of a state to "...observe, comply with, meet or perform any term, covenant, agreement, or other provision contained in this agreement."

## Administrative Costs Charged to SSBCI Were Not Allowable or Allocable

We found that $216,820 in administrative costs charged to the SSBCI program as of March 31, 2012, did not comply with program guidance. Section 4.2 of the Vermont Allocation Agreement states that the participating state shall only use the allocated funds for the purposes and activities specified in the agreement and for paying allowable costs of those purposes and activities in accordance with the cost principals set forth in OMB Circular A-87 (*Cost Principles for State, Local, and Indian Tribal Governments*) and codified in 2 C.F.R. part 235.

VEDA calculated and charged administrative costs to the SSBCI program using a "Fee for Service Model" based on the individual activities being performed on loans supported by SSBCI funds. These activities included servicing fees, origination fees, and closing fees. The fees charged were based on cost estimates rather than actual incurred costs. VEDA did not document the actual direct costs incurred or prepare a cost allocation plan (in accordance with OMB Circular A-87) that allocated the actual SSBCI incurred costs to its programs and activities. For example, VEDA did not maintain employee time sheets or other payroll records to show how much time employees worked on SSBCI activities.

Therefore, Treasury should disallow $216,820 in administrative expenses that Vermont associated with the SSBCI program unless the State can provide documentation showing actual expenses and how they were allocated to the SSBCI program in accordance with OMB Circular A-87. Treasury should also require that the State demonstrate it has a process to document actual costs incurred and a cost allocation plan for SSBCI before approving additional claims for administrative expenses.

## Vermont Did Not Obtain Borrower and Lender Assurances at Loan Closing

The Act and SSBCI Policy Guidelines require that lenders obtain borrower assurances that (1) loan proceeds will be used for approved business purposes, (2) loan proceeds will not be used for specifically prohibited purposes, (3) the borrower and lender are not related parties, (4) the borrower is not engaged in specifically prohibited activities, and (5) the principals of the borrowers have not been convicted of a sex offense against a minor.

Additionally, under the SSBCI Policy Guidelines, each state must obtain an assurance from the financial institution lender affirming that (1) the loan is not for prior debt that is not covered under the approved state program or that was owed to the lender or an affiliate of the lender, (2) the loan is not a refinancing of a loan previously made to the borrower by the lender or an affiliate of the lender, and (3) no principal of the lender has been convicted of a sex offense against a minor.[2] For each transaction, assurances must be completed and executed prior to the transfer of funds. While Vermont collected all the required borrower and lender assurances by the conclusion of our audit field work, 20 (or 77 percent) of the 26 loans reviewed were missing assurances at the time of loan closing.

We discussed the incomplete borrower and lender assurances with VEDA officials responsible for administering Vermont's other credit support programs during our audit entrance conference on March 13, 2012. VEDA officials explained that given the absence of a standard assurance form from Treasury, they had attempted to comply with requirements by designing their own assurance certifications based upon language in the Allocation Agreement. VEDA officials also told us they were not aware of the specific lender and borrower assurance requirements contained in the April 27, 2011, SSBCI Policy Guidelines.

Treasury relies on participating states to submit quarterly certifications that their SSBCI-funded programs are being implemented in accordance with requirements of the Act and Treasury guidelines. However, our audit demonstrated that although Vermont provided those certifications in September 2011, December 2011, and March 2012, Vermont's programs were not being implemented in accordance with all program requirements because the required assurances were incomplete. Moreover, the results show that the State did not collect the information needed to support its certifications to Treasury that its use of funds complied with program requirements. Therefore, it was not in compliance with Section 4.1 of its Allocation Agreement.

We believe that these events may constitute a general event of default under the Allocation Agreement because over half of the borrower

---

[2] Under Treasury's October 2011 guidelines, "principal" is defined as: the proprietor of a sole proprietorship; each partner in a partnership; each of the five most highly compensated executives, officers, or employees of a corporation, limited liability company, association, or a development company; or each direct or indirect holder of 20 percent or more of the ownership stock or stock equivalent of that entity.

assurances for the loans reviewed were incomplete prior to the loan closing dates. Under the Allocation Agreement signed by Vermont, Treasury, in its sole discretion, may find a state to be in default of its Allocation Agreement if the state materially fails to comply with, meet, or perform any term, covenant, agreement, or other provision contained in the agreement. Further, Treasury may also find a state to be in default under the Allocation Agreement if any representation or certification made to Treasury is found to be inaccurate, false, incomplete, or misleading in any material respect.

Based on our audit findings, we believe Vermont's September 2011 and December 2011 certifications of compliance were materially inaccurate. Additionally, because corrective actions to ensure that all borrower assurances had been obtained had not been implemented as of May 1, 2012, we believe Vermont's March 2012 certification may also be materially inaccurate. Although Vermont collected the missing assurances, we believe that the State's failure to initially collect the assurances and its inaccurate certifications may have triggered a general event of default under its Allocation Agreement. Therefore, Treasury should consider whether Vermont has satisfactorily cured its non-compliance issues or whether future funding to Vermont should be suspended, reduced, or terminated.

To strengthen states' accountability for compliance with SSBCI requirements, we made two prior recommendations, which Treasury subsequently implemented. In August 2011, we recommended that Treasury require borrowers and lenders to provide compliance assurances to designated state agencies responsible for administering the SSBCI funds, and require that participating states review them.[3] On March 6, 2012, Treasury issued *SSBCI National Standards for Compliance and Oversight*, which became effective on May 15, 2012. The standards say that Treasury expects participating states to establish a process to determine whether required borrower and lender certifications have been adequately documented. We believe that the standards, which were published in the Federal Register and emailed

---

[3] OIG-SBLF-11-002, STATE SMALL BUSINESS CREDIT INITIATIVE: Treasury Needs to Strengthen State Accountability for Use of Funds, August 5, 2011.

to all participating states, adequately inform participants of their responsibility for collecting and reviewing borrower and lender assurances.

We also recommended that Treasury either modify the Allocation Agreement or amend its policy guidelines to require participating states to make representations that they are monitoring and enforcing compliance with SSBCI Policy Guidelines and other program restrictions. Although Treasury initially declined to implement the recommendation, it has since issued national compliance standards for SSBCI that establish the oversight responsibilities of participating states and recommends a framework that states adopt for identifying, monitoring, and managing compliance risks. Therefore, we believe that generally Treasury has taken sufficient steps to strengthen states' accountability for the use of SSBCI funds.

## Recommendations

We recommend that the Deputy Assistant Secretary for Small Business, Housing and Community Development:

1) Disallow the entire $216,820 of administrative expenses claimed through March 31, 2012, unless the State provides documentation in accordance with OMB Circular A-87, showing actual expenses incurred and how they were allocated to the SSBCI program.

   **Management Response**

   Treasury agreed with this recommendation and said it would disallow the expenses.

   **OIG Comment**

   We consider Treasury's action to be responsive to our recommendation.

2) Require the State to provide a sub-accounting of all the funds transferred in connection with the interest rate subsidy program as well as program income generated by the use of such funds.

**Management Response**

Treasury agreed with this recommendation and will require that Vermont provide a sub-accounting of all the funds transferred as well as any program income generated.

**OIG Comment**

We consider Treasury's action to be responsive to our recommendation.

3) Require that the State demonstrate it has a system for tracking actual costs incurred and an SSBCI cost allocation plan before approving additional claims for administrative expenses.

**Management Response**

Treasury agreed with the recommendation, but also stated that Vermont will no longer charge any administrative expenses to SSBCI. However in the event that it charges administrative expenses in the future, Treasury will require Vermont to provide the necessary documentation.

**OIG Comment**

We consider Treasury's action to be responsive to our recommendation.

4) Determine whether there has been a general event of default under Vermont's Allocation Agreement resulting from the State's non-compliance with the grants management common rule or lender/borrower assurance requirements. If such an event has occurred and has not been adequately cured, determine whether it warrants a reduction, suspension, or termination of future funding to the State.

**Management Response**

Treasury agreed with this recommendation and will determine whether Vermont has adequately cured its noncompliance, and whether any further action is warranted.

**OIG Comment**

We consider Treasury's action to be responsive to our recommendation.

\* \* \* \* \* \*

We appreciate the courtesies and cooperation provided to our staff during the evaluation. If you wish to discuss the report, you may contact me at (202) 622-1090 or Lisa DeAngelis, Audit Director, at (202) 927-5621.

/s/
Debra Ritt
Special Deputy Inspector General for
Office of Small Business Lending Fund Program Oversight

# Appendix 1: Objective, Scope, and Methodology

The objective of our audit was to test participant compliance with program requirements and prohibitions to identify reckless or intentional misuse. As of March 31, 2012, Vermont had used or obligated approximately $2,582,172 in SSBCI funds through its Commercial Participation Program, Technology Participation Program, and the Small Business Participation Program. An additional program, the Vermont Financial Access Program, had not spent or obligated any funds in the period to December 31, 2011.

Our audit scope included small business loans enrolled in the SSBCI-supported programs from the date of Vermont's approval as an SSBCI participant, March 22, 2011, to December 31, 2011. During this period, VEDA made 36 loans with a total loan value of approximately $30 million. SSBCI funds totaling $2,083,640 were used in support of these loans.

We interviewed the management and staff of VEDA responsible for administering the SSBCI program on behalf of the State of Vermont. These interviews were conducted at VEDA offices in Vermont to understand and assess:

- Whether the State used its allocated funding under the program in accordance its approved application;

- Procedures in place to process small business loans and ensure compliance with the requirements of the Act and associated SSBCI Policy Guidelines; and

- Accounting and reporting processes, including methodologies for calculating and reporting administrative expenses.

In conjunction with the interviews, we also reviewed certain written policies, procedures, and guidance established by VEDA for administration of SSBCI funds. In addition, we statistically sampled 26 loans enrolled in Vermont's SSBCI programs as of December 31, 2011, and performed testing to ensure all loans complied with the requirements and prohibitions of the Act and associated Treasury guidelines. These loans were originated by 14 lending institutions throughout Vermont.

During June 2012, we conducted an on-site review of loan files at VEDA and compared the documentation to specific requirements and prohibitions of the Act and associated Treasury guidelines. The loan files supporting our review were provided by VEDA's staff.

We conducted our audit from June 2012 to October 2012 in accordance with Government Auditing Standards. Those standards require that we plan and perform the audit to obtain sufficient, appropriate evidence to provide a reasonable basis for our findings and conclusions based on our audit objectives. We believe that the evidence obtained to address our audit objectives provides a reasonable basis for our findings and conclusions.

# Appendix 2: Management Response

DEPARTMENT OF THE TREASURY
WASHINGTON, D.C. 20220

November 20, 2012

Debra Ritt
Special Deputy Inspector General for
 Office of Small Business Lending Fund Program Oversight
U.S. Department of the Treasury
1500 Pennsylvania Avenue, NW
Washington, DC 20220

Dear Ms. Ritt:

Thank you for the opportunity to review the Office of the Inspector General's (OIG) draft report entitled *Vermont's Use of Funds Received from the State Small Business Credit Initiative* (the Report). This letter provides the official response of the Department of the Treasury (Treasury).

With your consent, Treasury transmitted a revised draft of the Report to Vermont program officials on November 14, 2012. Treasury directed Vermont to submit a written reply describing the remedial measures it has taken or plans to take to address the deficiencies noted in the Report, including those related to collection of required lender and borrower assurances and the documentation of administrative costs.

Vermont's reply, enclosed, details steps Vermont has taken to improve program compliance with SSBCI policies and procedures. Among other things, Vermont states that borrower and lender assurances for all loans enrolled in SSBCI have been obtained, and that VEDA/VT has instituted a new SSBCI Reporting Procedure that will enhance monitoring of allocated funds employed and program income generated for all SSBCI enrolled loans. The reply also notes that "VEDA/VT has demonstrated good faith throughout its participation in the SSBCI program, including several dialogues with Treasury staff to discuss and modify practices to conform participation with Treasury directives."

Treasury agrees with the Report's first and third recommendations regarding $216,820 in administrative expenses. Vermont's reply states that those costs were charged based on a misunderstanding of the necessary documentation, and Treasury will disallow those expenses in accordance with OMB Circular No. A-87. Vermont also states that, prospectively, it will not charge any administrative expenses to the SSBCI funds. Treasury will require Vermont to provide necessary documentation in the event it does charge administrative expenses.

Treasury also agrees with the Report's second recommendation and will require that Vermont provide a sub-accounting of all the funds transferred in connection with the interest rate subsidy program as well as program income generated by the use of such funds. Treasury notes that incompatibilities between Vermont's accounting practices and SSBCI program requirements

1

occurred and were detected only after Treasury authorized the interest-rate subsidy program and were not apparent in Vermont's application to the program. As the Report further observes, earlier this year Treasury and Vermont modified the interest-rate program to address the issues identified in the Report.

Finally, Treasury concurs with the Report's fourth recommendation and will determine whether Vermont has adequately cured its noncompliance with financial institution lender and small business borrower assurance requirements. We appreciate that the Report acknowledges "updated borrower and lender assurances in the correct format for all of the closed loans [OIG] tested had been received by the conclusion of [the OIG] audit field work." Treasury will also determine whether any further action is warranted.

Thank you once again for the opportunity to review the Report. Treasury appreciates our work together throughout the course of the SSBCI program.

Sincerely,

Don Graves, Jr.
Deputy Assistant Secretary for Small Business, Community Development, and Affordable Housing Policy

Enclosure

**VERMONT ECONOMIC DEVELOPMENT AUTHORITY**

Vermont Agricultural Credit Corporation
Vermont Small Business Loan Program
Vermont 504 Corporation

November 19, 2012

Clifton G. Kellogg, Director of State Small Business Credit Initiative
Department of the Treasury
Sent Via Email: Clifton.Kellogg@treasury.gov

RE:  Vermont Economic Development Authority ("VEDA/VT")

Dear Cliff:

This is in reply to your letter dated November 14, 2012 which transmitted a copy of the Department of the Treasury Office of Inspection General draft report ("OIG Report").

VEDA/VT's narrative response to the OIG Report is attached. We appreciate the opportunity to respond to the issues raised by the OIG Report. If further clarification or a supplemental response is required, please contact me directly. As indicated in the narrative, the sub-accounting referenced in your letter is being provided under separate cover.

Thank you.

Very truly yours,

Rosalea W. Bradley
Chief Executive Officer

VEDA: TEL (802) 828-5627  VACC: (866) 828-3276  FAX: (802) 828-5474
58 EAST STATE STREET, SUITE 5, MONTPELIER, VERMONT 05602-3044

SSBCI Narrative Response - 1

## NARRATIVE RESPONSE TO THE TREASURY OFFICE OF THE INSPECTOR GENERAL (OIG) DRAFT REPORT ENTITLED "VERMONT'S USE OF FUNDS RECEIVED FROM THE STATE SMALL BUSINESS CREDIT INITIATIVE."

**TREASURY REQUEST 1.** Provide the documentation requested in Recommendation 1 of the Report with respect to administrative expenses and a description of previous, current, or planned efforts to improve internal controls to ensure all Allocated Funds are used for authorized purposes as described in Section 4.2 of the Allocation Agreement.

RESPONSE:

Treasury's *Guidelines* (October, 2011) and Section 4.2 of the Allocation Agreement stipulate that States comply with OMB Circular A-87 ("OMB A-87"). Accordingly, VEDA/VT prepared and implemented a Fee-for-Service Cost Allocation Plan (the "Plan"), certified by the Authority's Chief Financial Officer as compliant with OMB A-87. This Plan represented a good faith effort to comply with plans believed to be permissible and encouraged under OMB A-87. [2 CFR Part 2, Appendix A, A. Purpose and Scope 2.b]

However, upon publication of the *SSBCI National Standards for Compliance and Oversight* in March 2012, effective May 15, 2012, it became clear to VEDA/VT that direct costing (i.e. time cards, specific hours applied) was required. Consequently, VEDA/VT made the decision (with approval of Treasury) to amend its quarterly reports for September 30, 2011, December 31, 2011 and March 31, 2012 and remove 100% of the administrative costs claimed on the reports.

VEDA/VT has no plans to use Allocated Funds for administrative costs prospectively if tracking of direct costs is required.

**TREASURY REQUEST 2.** Provide a sub-accounting of the use of Allocated Funds and program income generated in the Commercial Loan Participation Program.

RESPONSE:

VEDA/VT acknowledges the incompatibility of its interest rate subsidy program accounting system with the reporting requirements of the SSBCI program, a reality neither Treasury nor VEDA/VT recognized when the program was initiated. VEDA/VT strongly disputes any assertion that this system is insufficient or inadequate in any other context or application other than SSBCI. Moreover, VEDA/VT's estimate of the SSBCI funds to be used in the future to subsidize amortizing loans are in our view "obligated" as that term is defined by Treasury Guidelines. Accordingly, VEDA/VT is at a loss as to how this practice can be characterized as a breach of the Allocation Agreement.

VEDA: TEL (802) 828-5627 VACC: (866) 828-3276 FAX: (802) 828-5474
58 EAST STATE STREET, SUITE 5, MONTPELIER, VERMONT 05602-3044

SSBCI Narrative Response - 2

Effective September 30, 2012, VEDA/VT instituted a new SSBCI Reporting Procedure which enables its loan accounting system to monthly report the total Allocated Funds employed and program income generated for all SSBCI enrolled loans (individually and in aggregate) in accordance with Treasury Guidelines. OIG has reviewed this Reporting Procedure and found it to be satisfactory for audit purposes. The sub-accounting which employs this procedure is being delivered to Treasury under separate cover as it contains confidential borrower information unsuitable for publication and consists of 3 components:

    a. An EXCEL workbook, with multiple spreadsheets that interface to the VEDA's loan accounting system and perform the calculations to determine the amount of Allocated Funds and Program Income used;

    b. A written procedure to document the components of the EXCEL workbook as well as the on-line reporting to Treasury;

    c. A reconciliation of the restricted cash account;

**TREASURY REQUEST 3.** **Describe any previous, current, or planned efforts to develop a system for tracking actual administrative costs based on a cost allocation plan.**

RESPONSE:

As noted previously, VEDA/VT has elected to use 100% of VEDA/VT's $13.2 million allocation for funding eligible loans and will not use SSBCI funds for administration costs as long as direct costing is required. Accordingly, no response is necessary.

**TREASURY REQUEST 4.** **Describe any previous, current, or planned efforts to improve internal controls to ensure that all borrower and lender assurances are collected at the time of closing each transaction.**

RESPONSE:

VEDA/VT acknowledges full compliance with all Policy Guideline requirements for written borrower and lender assurances was not attained until June 13, 2012. Nevertheless, it is submitted that VEDA/VT's intervening efforts and interim measures, including the cure of all noncompliant loan files contemporaneous with conclusion of the OIG audit field work, merit consideration.

VEDA/VT is a seasoned lender, having been formed in 1974 by act of the Vermont legislature as a "body corporate and politic and a public instrumentality of the state" [10 VSA §213(a)] authorized to provide funding, usually in concert with private lenders, to industrial, commercial or agricultural enterprises. Representations, assurances and certifications are required from every Borrower and VEDA/VT long ago standardized the methodology for obtaining same through direct inclusion in loan agreements, promissory notes, mortgage and security instruments, guaranties, and related closing instruments. Accordingly, VEDA/VT was tardy in recognizing that the independent assurances and certifications referenced in the Allocation

VEDA: TEL (802) 828-5627 VACC: (866) 828-3276 FAX: (802) 828-5474
58 EAST STATE STREET, SUITE 5, MONTPELIER, VERMONT 05602-3044

SSBCI Narrative Response - 3

Agreement would have to be obtained through independent documentation. An immediate effort was undertaken to prepare and implement documentation based upon VEDA/VT's extensive experience but it wasn't until early spring of 2012 that lender and borrower assurances based upon the precise letter of Policy Guidelines and FAQ were implemented. In due course, and with great diligence and speed, assurances were pursued with respect to every SSBCI project such that the closed loans tested by OIG were confirmed as assurance compliant by the close of the OIG's audit field work.

Consistent with its role as an established lender, VEDA/VT fully recognizes the responsibility to fully comply with the requirements of loan documentation. Had there been specimen forms of approved assurances for lenders and borrowers attached as exhibits to the Allocation Agreement there is no question but that VEDA/VT would have avoided tardy compliance and little doubt that from inception of the SSBCI program each and every loan file would have had the requisite assurances at closing. Otherwise, the loan would not have closed. The Allocation Agreement anticipates that under appropriate circumstances Treasury may, in the exercise of its sound discretion, refrain from both declaring a default and imposing remedies. VEDA/VT has demonstrated good faith throughout its participation in the SSBCI program, including several dialogues with Treasury staff to discuss and modify practices to conform participation with Treasury directives. Moreover, the substance of the OIG report recognizes this good faith in several instances, including a clear intention and willingness to reach full compliance immediately without delay and without resort to compulsive directives.

As of the date hereof, borrower and lender assurances for all loans enrolled in the SSBCI have been obtained.

VEDA: TEL (802) 828-5627 VACC: (866) 828-3276 FAX: (802) 828-5474
58 EAST STATE STREET, SUITE 5, MONTPELIER, VERMONT 05602-3044

## Appendix 3: Major Contributors

Debra Ritt, Special Deputy Inspector General

Lisa DeAngelis, Audit Director

Clayton Boyce, Audit Director

John Rizek, Supervisory Auditor

Andrew Morgan, Auditor

Safal Bhattarai, Auditor

## Appendix 4: Distribution List

### Department of the Treasury
Deputy Secretary
Office of Strategic Planning and Performance Management
Risk and Control Group

### Office of Management and Budget
OIG Budget Examiner

### United States Senate
Chairman and Ranking Member
Committee on Small Business and Entrepreneurship

Chairman and Ranking Member
Committee on Finance

Chairman and Ranking Member
Committee on Banking, Housing, and Urban Affairs

### United States House of Representatives
Chairman and Ranking Member
Committee on Small Business

Chairman and Ranking Member
Committee on Financial Services

### Government Accountability Office
Comptroller General of the United States

www.ingramcontent.com/pod-product-compliance
Lightning Source LLC
Chambersburg PA
CBHW081818170526
45167CB00008B/3453